Zodiac Signs

All about zodiac signs and astrology, how they work, how to use them for success, horoscopes, and more!

Table Of Contents

Introduction 1
Chapter 1: Understanding Astrology 2
Chapter 2: The 12 Signs of the Zodiac 4
Chapter 3: The Planets and Planet Signs 10
Chapter 4: The 12 Houses 16
Chapter 5: Planetary Transits 19
Chapter 6: Deciphering Your Destiny 21
Conclusion 24

Introduction

I want to thank you and congratulate you for downloading the book, "Zodiac Signs'.

This book contains helpful information about Zodiac signs, what they are, and how they work!

You will soon discover exactly how the science of Astrology works, including its history, the different Zodiac signs, their meanings, movements, and what it all means with regard to your life!

Astrology and the use of Zodiac signs has been around for thousands of years. Over time it has been developed into an articulated science that can accurately predict events and behaviors.

Whether you're a skeptic or not, this book will give you a great understanding of the complicated skills required to be an astrologer.

This book will also explain to you tips and techniques that will allow you to successfully understand and begin using zodiac signs to improve your life!

If you're new to Astrology, or have been implementing it for some time, this book will have something to offer you in the way of insight, knowledge, power, and entertainment.

Thanks again for downloading this book, I hope you enjoy it!

Chapter 1:
Understanding Astrology

Astrology is the science of how the planets, stars, satellites (i.e. the planets' moons), comets, and other heavenly bodies affect our personalities and destinies. Now before you laugh and toss this book away because I had the audacity to call astrology a science, let me clarify that I use the term 'science' to mean an *organized and logical* study of a subject. I prefer to use this term because it highlights the fact that astrology is not something that a bunch of hippies from the 1960s simply made up while they were all high.

In fact, the science of astrology is centuries old. It started when the Ancient Babylonians noticed that the movements of the heavenly bodies are not random but follow regular patterns. Further, these movements have an effect on the personalities of people, what likely happens to them, and many others. After several centuries of studying these patterns and their effects, we now have a better understanding of astrology and how this kind of knowledge can improve our lives.

If you are truly serious about using astrology to improve your life, you must hire the services of a professional astrologer and ask them to read your chart. There are many possible charts they can make and read for you, e.g. your birth chart which focuses on your personality or who you are, your planetary transits to know what the year will bring, a reading focused on your career, romance or family life, etc.

It is also possible to make your own reading even if you only have a basic understanding of astrology, but it is very likely that you will only make very general judgments. A professional astrologer will be able to give you the nitty-gritty details, e.g. when you will be married, if you will ever be divorced, etc., and the readings are usually about 70-90% accurate.

Only 70-90% accurate? That is actually not bad. Take note that astrology, like psychiatry and medical science, cannot always be 100% accurate because there are many factors involved in their field of study. A psychiatrist or medical doctor can zero in on the major factors involved in a case, but there will always be some minor factor that can influence a case.

If you attempt to make your own reading, and you are not a professional astrologer, your readings will probably be only 30-50% accurate. Further, it must be reiterated that your interpretations will probably very general, e.g. 'there is romance in the air,' as opposed to 'you will definitely get married.' Please take this into consideration when you attempt to read your own charts.

Of course, the more you know about astrology, the more accurate your readings will be. Before that happens, you must know the basics.

Chapter 2:
The 12 Signs of the Zodiac

The term 'zodiac' refers to the circle of the universe surrounding the Earth divided into 12 equal areas measuring 30° each. To help you understand this, draw a circle and make it as perfect as possible. You will not understand this if you create an oblong. In the center of that circle, make a dot. That dot represents the planet Earth and the area inside the circle represents the heavens where the planetary bodies reside. Now divide the circle into 12 equal slices. What you have drawn is a simple representation of the zodiac.

Please always keep the image of the Earth in the center and the heavens surrounding it in your mind. Astrology always views reality from the Earth because this is where we live. If we lived on Venus, then our astrology would be understood according to the view from the planet Venus.

According to astrology, each of the 12 slices in the zodiac circle has its own distinct characteristics. They are represented by the 12 zodiac signs and their symbols:

1. Aries the ram

2. Taurus the bull

3. Gemini the twins

4. Cancer the crab

5. Leo the lion

6. Virgo the maiden

7. Libra the scales

8. Scorpio the scorpion

9. Sagittarius the centaur archer

10. Capricorn the sea-goat, a goat with the tail of a fish

11. Aquarius the water-bearer

12. Pisces the fish

These 12 signs are fixed in the circle of the heavens and they only move when the heavens itself moves or when the Earth moves. To understand this, go back to your drawing. The 12 slices will not move unless you move the paper around. Even so, the 12 slices do not move *within* the circle but are stable. Now get a penny or small circle of paper to represent the Earth and make a small dot on the edge to represent where you are on the Earth. If you move this penny, from your point of view on Earth, the 12 signs also seem to move.

The 12 signs influence the planets which happen to be in that area. The planets include the following: sun, moon, Mercury, Venus, Mars, Jupiter, Saturn, Neptune, Uranus, and Pluto. Astrology also considers the satellites, comets, etc., but they play a lesser role compared to the planets. In fact, some astrologers usually do not bother with them.

The sun and moon are considered planets in astrology because, as we have explained, astrology is understood from the Earth, and from this point of view the sun and moon revolve around the Earth.

The basic premise of astrology is that the heavenly bodies influence our personalities, and destinies. How they do this will depend on where the planets are located in the zodiac circle. For example, if the sun is located in Scorpio, then its influence will be tainted by the characteristics of Scorpio.

To help you understand this, imagine that your personality or destiny is a theater play. In every play, there will be characters and the actors who play them. The director's choice of actor will influence how the character is portrayed in the play. For example, an actor who acts in a comedic way, like Hugh Grant, will always give a hint of comedy in all the characters he portrays even if the character as created by the playwright is not necessarily comedic.

With this in mind, let us consider the 'characters' of the 12 signs:

1. Aries the ram – independent, optimistic, impulsive and impatient. Aries is like a child who carelessly runs across a field without thinking about the possible dangers behind every bush.

2. Taurus the bull – dependable, loyal, stubborn and materialistic. Taurus is like your responsible but old-fashioned father who will always bring home the bacon but will not be persuaded to open a Facebook account.

3. Gemini the twins – imaginative, witty, impulsive and indecisive. Gemini is someone who runs with Aries across the field, but stops to make a wreath of wildflowers only to abandon it halfway. Alternatively, Gemini is like a boss who comes up with several wild goals, but leaves it to his employees to figure out how to achieve them.

4. Cancer the crab – maternal, caring, sensitive and moody. Cancer is like the ultimate mother who gives you cookies and milk after school.

5. Leo the lion – confident, ambitious, domineering and showy. Leo is the queen bee who likes to show off but at the same time wants you to really like her for who she is.

6. Virgo the maiden – logical, observant, fussy and meddlesome. Virgo is the know-it-all who always comments on various aspects about your life, but only because she has a genuine concern for your well-being.

7. Libra the scales – diplomatic, friendly, indecisive and changeable. Libra is the peace-maker who always tries to accommodate everyone's pizza topping preference even if it leads to disastrous results: anchovies, mushrooms, pineapple and … shredded coconut?

8. Scorpio the scorpion – passionate, observant, manipulative and possessive. Scorpio is like Virgo, but before he tells you what you need to do to improve your life, he will first give you a look of disdain then spend months trying to decide if he cares enough about you to *waste* his time trying to improve you.

9. Sagittarius the centaur archer - independent, adventurous, overly-optimistic and easily bored. Sagittarius is like Gemini, but instead of leaving his projects half-finished, he commits himself 100% to it, *and* to all related projects. E.g. Sagittarius says, 'After this flower wreath, let us plant a flower garden and start a flower business and …'

10. Capricorn the sea-goat – ambitious, practical, pessimistic and stubborn. Capricorn is like the Taurus dad, but unlike Taurus who is usually satisfied with a boring job as long as it pays well, they want to become the CEO.

11. Aquarius the water-bearer – witty, innovative, rebellious and aloof. Aquarius is like your hippie sister who, instead of accepting a scholarship to Harvard Law School, joined the Peace Corps and is now selling organic soaps made from some obscure oil only found in some obscure island in the South Pacific. She also just broke up with her boyfriend, but doesn't seem to be heartbroken.

12. Pisces the fish – imaginative, compassionate, lazy and prone to fantasies. Pisces is your other hippie sister who never bothered with college applications, who always dreams of writing poetry but never attempts to do so, and who always joins your Cancer mother in baking cookies.

Take note that these descriptions are generalizations. I have only considered the most obvious characteristics, but, like all characterizations, there is always more than meets the eye.

Also, although I used caricatures of persons to describe the 12 signs, I do not wish to imply that the 12 signs are like persons. I simply chose to use these descriptions because I think they are the easiest to understand. Some astrologers use places to describe these signs, e.g. Cancer is like a Connecticut suburb while Scorpio is like a red light district in Thailand, etc. It is certainly also possible to use other similes as well.

Further, if, while reading the above descriptions, you say that you don't agree at all because you are an Aquarius but your personality is very far from the hippie sister I've described above, that is because I am *not* describing a person with an Aquarius sun sign, rather I am only describing the Aquarius part of the zodiac circle using caricatures of persons. To explain all of this further, let us proceed to the next chapter on planets.

Chapter 3:
The Planets and Planet Signs

In the previous chapter, we discussed that the planets are the actors while the signs they are found in are the characters they play. To understand how everything is connected, let us now discuss the planets themselves and what each 'actor' is like.

1. Sun – the brightest personality in the room.

2. Moon – the introverted shy friend who always stays in the background.

3. Mercury – a talkative, extroverted person who always has something to say about everything.

4. Venus – the shrewd, intelligent and extremely attractive beauty queen.

5. Mars – the shrewd, intelligent and extremely attractive star athlete.

6. Jupiter – the jovial and generous neighbor who never seems to run into any bad luck.

7. Saturn – the stern grandfather who never smiles and who always wants to know how you are doing in life.

8. Neptune – the dreamy artist who always makes incomprehensible abstract art which inexplicably almost always sells for millions.

9. Uranus – the innovator who is always thinking of new things to create.

10. Pluto – the police detective with penetrating eyes.

If you have not yet noticed, the characters of these planets seem to have their twin in the 12 zodiac signs. For instance, if the brightest personality is the queen bee and Leo is like the queen bee, is there some connection between the zodiac sign Leo and the sun?

There is indeed a connection which led to astrologers relating these 10 planets with the 12 zodiac signs. If the planets are the actors and the zodiac signs are the characters in a drama, then the sun with its bright personality will give its best performance if it is in the zodiac sign Leo. In other words, the sun will be most like the sun if it is a Leo sun.

Here are the pairings:

1. Sun – Leo

2. Moon – Cancer

3. Mercury – Gemini and Virgo

4. Venus – Taurus and Libra

5. Mars – Aries and Scorpio

6. Jupiter – Sagittarius and Pisces

7. Saturn – Capricorn and Aquarius

8. Neptune – Pisces

9. Uranus – Aquarius

10. Pluto – Scorpio

We call these pairings 'planetary rulings,' e.g. the planetary ruler of Leo is the sun. However, do not think that the sun rules the sign of Leo in the same sense as a king does, as if a planet can rule that slice of space in the circular horizon. The term 'planetary ruler' is a technical term in astrology which has significance when understanding your destiny. Let us park this term for the meantime until we get to chapters 5 and 6.

Some of the planets rule 2 signs because there are only 10 planets but there are 12 signs. However, some of the signs have 2 planetary rulers because there used to be a time when astronomers (those who study the physical movements of the heavenly bodies and the universe) had not yet discovered some of the outer planets. For example, Pluto was only discovered in the 1930s, hence the ancient astronomers could not have possibly assigned it as Scorpio's ruler. In the future, if astronomers discover new planets in our solar system after Pluto, some of the zodiac signs might come to have 2 planetary rulers as well.

If a sign has 2 planetary rulers, one is considered the ancient ruler and the other the modern ruler. The 3 outer planets Neptune, Uranus and Pluto are the modern rulers of Pisces, Aquarius and Scorpio respectively.

There are 2 ways to understand the role of planets in astrology and these will depend on what we are trying to understand. Generally speaking, in astrology, either you are trying to know yourself, i.e. your personality, or trying to know what will happen to you, i.e. your destiny.

To know your personality, you must know *all* your planet signs or the positions of all the planets at the time of your birth depending on where you are on the planet. To know your destiny, you must also know the general position of the planets in the heavens regardless where you currently are on Earth.

For now, it would be too complicated to discuss the second without first discussing the 12 houses, so let us park that for a moment until we get to the last chapters. In this chapter, let us focus on the planetary signs.

When people speak of their zodiac sign, they are referring to their sun sign or the sign where the sun is located at the time of their birth depending on the place of their birth. For many people, reading about their sun sign is good enough because they can relate to most of it. For example, most Scorpios will agree that they are obsessive.

However, the sun sign only shows 60% of your personality. The rest will be provided by the other planetary signs.

Here are the aspects of your personality determined by each of the planets:

1. Sun – your core self

2. Moon – your emotions

3. Mercury – the way you communicate

4. Venus – the way you love

5. Mars – how aggressive you are or how you try to achieve your goals

6. Jupiter – how you express your generosity

7. Saturn – your serious side

8. Neptune – your dreamy side or the part of you which day-dreams

9. Uranus – your impulsive and innovative side

10. Pluto – your unconscious emotions

If you have a complete list of all of your planet signs, you will have a complete understanding of your personality. In advanced astrology, the exact degree is also noted since this will further tweak your understanding. For example, Pluto in 0° Scorpio, i.e. the part of the heavens when Libra transitions to Scorpio, will exhibit less Scorpio characteristics than a Pluto that is in 15° Scorpio. You must also consider the relationships between the planets, e.g. if the distance between Saturn and Jupiter is 10° or less, if they are at opposite sides of the zodiac circle, etc. to further get into the nitty-gritty of things.

To show the importance of planet signs, consider this example: sun sign Cancer, moon sign Aquarius, Mercury sign Gemini and Venus sign Scorpio. This person will likely be very maternal and caring, but he will not be affected much if another person does not seem to appreciate his efforts because with a moon in Aquarius, he is detached from his emotions. He can be quite chatty with his friends and colleagues due to his Mercury being in Gemini, but when it comes to his wife or girlfriend, he is seductive and sly because his Venus is in Scorpio.

Now let's consider a different Cancer with her moon sign in Scorpio, Mercury in Capricorn and Venus in Virgo. This person will be maternal and caring, but she easily becomes moody and vindictive when people don't reciprocate her efforts due to her moon being in Scorpio. When conversing, she refrains from mentioning mundane matters due to her Mercury in Capricorn. In love, she believes that showing is more important than doing, hence she will show her love by paying for her lover's gym membership so the latter can finally lose those last 10 pounds.

If you would like to know yourself better through a thorough analysis of your birth chart, I suggest seeking the services of a professional astrologist. If you are fine with a more general picture, there are internet sources which can calculate your birth chart for free, and then give you a general description of yourself based on the planet signs.

For many people, this in-depth understanding of the self is astrology's most important use. For example, if, due to a strong Pisces influence in your chart, you know that you are prone to day-dreaming and never follow-though, then you can try to *consciously* minimize this tendency. An astrological personality reading must not be understood to mean that you are who you are and can never improve yourself. While it is true that some people are more day-dreamers than dream-pursuers, they don't have to succumb to that destiny. It is possible to improve your weak points.

Not only can you improve yourself with astrology, but you can also help to improve other people. For example, by reading your children's birth chart, you will know how to effectively raise them.

What about the other general uses of astrology regarding the reading of destinies? Before we get into that, we must consider the 12 houses in the zodiac.

Chapter 4:
The 12 Houses

A complete birth chart will inform you of your planet signs and the houses where each planet falls. Recall that the planets are the actors in a theater play and the signs are the characters. Using the same analogy, when we speak of the houses, we are referring to the settings or the situations where the actors must project their character.

The houses represent the aspects in life which the planets will affect. To explain this, let us first look at the 12 houses:

1. Your ego or personality

2. Material possessions,

3. Communications, e.g. writing, speaking, and relationships with siblings

4. Home life

5. Creativity

6. Health and daily work habits

7. Marriage and partnerships, e.g. business partnerships

8. Death and sex

9. Higher education

10. Career

11. Hopes, wishes and friendships

12. The unconscious or the repressed self

To explain the roles of the houses, let us go back to the example used in the previous chapter: sun sign Cancer, moon sign Aquarius, Mercury sign Gemini and Venus sign Scorpio. This person's life will be influenced by the houses where these planets are located.

For instance, if the sun is in the 10th house, then, since the sun is like the brightest person in the room and represents the core self, this person will either consider his career to be important, or circumstances will influence him to make his career important. How exactly this happens will depend on the details of his life.

If the sun is in the 4th house, he will consider his home life to be more important, or circumstances will influence him to make it more important.

Regardless which house the sun is located, since it is a Cancer sun, the way this person deals with those matters, either career or home life, will be in a maternal and caring Cancerian way.

To give another example, if the moon is in the 3rd house, then, since the moon is like a shy introvert and represents the emotions, this person will likely have a quiet but emotional relationship with his siblings, or circumstances will influence this relationship to become like this.

If the moon is in the 7th house, then marriage and other partnerships will be a quiet but emotional one, or circumstances will influence the relationship to be like this.

Regardless of which house the moon is located, since it is an Aquarius moon, the person seems detached when it comes to his emotions, i.e. though he is capable of expressing and feeling emotions, he is also very logical about them and doesn't allow them to overcome him.

Notice that I always include the phrase 'circumstances will influence this aspect to be like this.' This is because the position of the planets in the houses can either indicate an additional detail in the personality or show what can happen later in life.

For example, a child who is born with a lot of planets in the 10th house may start out as a happy-go-lucky child who doesn't seem to have any ambition. Later, circumstances will influence this child to focus his energies on his career. What these circumstances will be will depend on the details of his life, but here is an example how this might come about: Let us say the child's parents once lost their jobs and the family never recovered financially. This influenced the child to want a successful career so as to never experience financial problems again.

People whose planets are equally distributed in the 12 houses will likely only experience minor changes and/or challenges in those aspects. Those who have a lot of planets in one house will likely experience major changes and/or challenges in that aspect. For the houses which are empty or have no planets in them, these are the relatively quiet aspects of your life. For example, if you have no planets in the 2nd house, then you will probably have no or very few minor changes and/or challenges regarding your material possessions.

Chapter 5:
Planetary Transits

Planetary transits refer to the path a planet takes through the heavens in the course of a set time. The planets in the solar system constantly move and this can be tracked by either astronomers or astrologers. Usually, the latter uses the calculations of the former and, based on this data, will announce the current planetary transits.

For example, an astrologer may announce that in this month, Venus is in Scorpio until the 28th, then it will move to Sagittarius on the 29th. The planets closer to the Earth move through the 12 zodiac signs quickly, but the larger planets will take years to move through each sign. For example, Saturn takes about 2 ½ years to transit each sign.

Transits will tell you what will happen during that time. For example, if Venus is in your sun sign, this usually means you become more attractive or more likely to experience romance. Meanwhile, if Saturn is in your sun sign, since this planet is like the stern grandfather who is always concerned about your well-being, perhaps you will experience some difficult challenges which are put there to improve yourself. This also applies to all the planetary signs. For example, if Saturn is in your Venus sign, since your Venus sign refers to the way you love, you might find yourself being more disciplined and cautious when it comes to romance.

The planetary ruler of each sign becomes significant when we talk of planetary transits. For example, let us say that Saturn is currently in Libra, and your Mercury sign is Capricorn. Saturn is the ruler of Capricorn, and your Mercury sign refers to the way you communicate. While Saturn is in Libra, you will become more Libran in the way you communicate, i.e. more diplomatic or balanced. However, you will not become completely Libran. Think of your Capricorn Mercury sign as a cup of coffee and the Libran influence as the dash of cinnamon on top.

Alternatively, the planetary transit may bring circumstances which force you to become more Libran in nature when it comes to how you communicate. For example, while Saturn is in Libra, if your Mercury sign is Capricorn, you might find yourself in situations where you must learn how to communicate with diplomacy. Perhaps you will become an arbiter for feuding relatives or colleagues.

The way planetary transits affect you will depend on *all* your planet signs. If you understand this, you will understand as well that the horoscope readings found in newspapers and magazines are too general to mean anything. These readings are based only on how the transits affect the sun sign, hence they will always be incomplete and too generalized to mean anything significant.

To understand how planetary transits affect you, you must study your birth chart carefully and update yourself with the current transits. Most astrology sites will provide this information for free.

Chapter 6: Deciphering Your Destiny

The previous chapters were quite lengthy, but they needed to be so in order to make you understand this chapter. Now that you have a basic understanding of astrology, you can understand how it can help you to know what your destiny or future is.

Let us first clarify that from the point of view of astrology, knowing a person's destiny or future is not necessarily incompatible with free will. Rather, a person's destiny is based on their personality. To explain this, think of a career you would probably never choose even if it makes you rich, e.g. a prostitute or criminal. If it is not in your personality to become either of those, or if it is not in your personality to want to be rich, then you will never become a prostitute or criminal. Instead, your destiny will always be based on who you are. Are you creative? Perhaps your destiny is to be an artist. If you are not creative, then your destiny cannot be to become an artist.

From the point of view of astrology, your destiny refers to what you were born to do or become. The circumstances or challenges which influence you to change course are only there to ensure that you indeed fulfill this destiny. Theoretically speaking, you *can* resist your destiny, but that would be irrational because your destiny is whatever it is that would make you feel fulfilled. Resisting your destiny is like deliberately wearing ill-fitting clothes even if properly-fitting clothes are right there beside you. From this point of view, those who are sad or disappointed in life are those who have resisted the lessons life has tried to teach them. For example, if you know from the very depths of your soul that you love someone, but always resist the urge to reach out even if life gives you several opportunities to do so, then you have nobody to blame but yourself when this person ends up marrying someone else.

If you know what your destiny is as determined by a thorough reading of your birth chart, you will know what you are supposed to do in life and will likely not doubt your instincts. For example, if your birth chart shows many planets in your 4th house, and this tells you that you value your home life the most, you will not doubt whether you should have been more aggressive when it came to your career. Instead, you will tell yourself that this is who you are and this will make you feel fulfilled.

Further, regarding transits, if you know the movements of the planets and how they influence you, then either you can take advantage of their influences or adopt your plans accordingly. For example, if Venus will be in your sun sign next month, and you know that this means you will become more susceptible to romance, then you should probably take your lover on a romantic getaway.

You can also prepare for major changes and possible challenges according to the planetary transits. Saturn transits usually indicate major life changes. Pluto transits indicate that difficult truths will soon come to light. Uranus transits indicate unexpected but transitory changes, e.g. the prim and proper lady suddenly takes a wild lover. Jupiter transits indicate where you will be lucky. Mars transits indicate where some major action will happen. Venus transits indicate romance. Mercury transits indicate issues with communications. Moon transits influence the state of your emotions or what will make you emotional. Sun transits influence the general feel of things, e.g. when the sun is in Aquarius, everything has a hint of Aquarian nature.

As I have mentioned before, the best way to benefit from astrology is to seek the services of a professional astrologer. I am not saying this only because I want you to spend money, after all astrological services are not cheap; rather, I am saying this because astrology is too complicated to be completely understood by a casual reader. Remember that it is an organized and logical study, just like medicine, engineering, physics, and so on. You cannot expect to read just one book on medicine then expect to be able to replace your local general practitioner. Professional astrologers, at least the good ones, have graduate degrees or at least have trained under other professional astrologers for several years.

If you hire a professional, you will be amazed at what they will be able to tell you. It will be more accurate than what you or any casual wanna-be astrologer will come up with, and your money will be very well-spent. Otherwise, if you are fine with a more general reading, then you must obtain a copy of your birth chart and be updated with the planetary transits.

Conclusion

Thank you again for downloading this book!

I hope this book was able to help you learn more about Zodiac signs and Astrology!

The next step is to put this information to use, and begin using the power of zodiac signs to your advantage, and understand how the planets are affecting your life!

Finally, if you enjoyed this book, please take the time to share your thoughts and post a review on Amazon. It'd be greatly appreciated!

Thank you and good luck!

www.ingramcontent.com/pod-product-compliance
Lightning Source LLC
LaVergne TN
LVHW021750060526
838200LV00052B/3564